Clive Oseman is a Brummie spoken word artist now based in Swindon, where he moved for work in 2003. He has been writing poetry for around fifteen years and was widely published worldwide, particularly in short-form journals and anthologies, before discovering performance poetry in 2014.

After early nerve-racked open-mic performances around the Bristol scene he got hooked on performance and now headlines, features and slams around the UK as well as co-hosting Oooh Beehive, Swindon's biggest regular spoken word event. The spoken word scene has transformed his life after a troubled childhood and serious illness left him withdrawn and painfully shy.

He is a keen sports fan with a particular love of rugby league and Birmingham City FC, and keenly political, being a member of the Labour Party and Momentum. Most importantly of all, he is the proud father of a wonderful daughter, Germaine, to whom this book is dedicated.

LIFE

Clive Oseman

Bx3

Copyright © 2018 Clive Oseman

The author asserts the moral right under the Copyright, Designs and Patents Act 1988 to be identified as the author of this work.

All rights reserved. No part of this publication may be reproduced, stored in a retrieval system, or transmitted, in any form or by any means without the prior written consent of the author, nor be otherwise circulated in any form of binding or cover other than that in which it is published and without a similar condition being imposed on the subsequent purchaser.

This edition published by Bx3, an imprint of Burning Eye Books 2018

www.burningeye.co.uk

@burningeyebooks

Burning Eye Books
15 West Hill, Portishead, BS20 6LG

ISBN 978-1-911570-61-5

*To Germaine.
You make me a very proud father.*

CONTENTS

Life	9
Not Your Clone	10
An As Yet Untitled Bit of 4am Can't Sleep Madness (Yes, That Is Now the Title)	14
The Future's Bright…	16
Six	19
No Greater Good	21
A Better World	23
Nearly Home?	25
The Art of Loving (Someone Who Likes You)	26
The Thief and the Suitcase	27
Bah, Humbug	29
Regrets	31
Deterrent	33
Noise	35
Not Right	36
Sweet	38
Impartial	39
Nothing Is Real	42
If…	44
Night and Day	45
What's Your Emergency? (2020)	46
Colin	48
Arson	49
Bill	50

Blame	52
Holding On	53
It's Over	55
Innocence	56
The Tower	57
Technique	59
Temptation	60
All the Same	62
Music	64
How to Be Like Me	65
School Report	67
Worthwhile?	69
Uneasy	70
Codeine Dreams	72
Dreaming	73
Truth	75
#RefugeesWelcome	76
The Real Message of the Harry Potter Story	77
Spoken Word	79
Last Request	82

LIFE

The very act of living
is like drinking from a broken bottle.
Get it right, the liquid is sublime,
sometimes the highs can't be described.

Get it wrong, catch the jagged edges
of deceit from those who use you,
love those who will abuse you,
and the scars are deep and permanent.

But you only have one bottle.
The suffering of the uncut risk-averse
is invisible but often worse
than the damage risked to quench a thirst.

The loneliness of dehydration
is as bad as fate can be.
Take the plunge and gulp it down.
Don't waste it all like me.

NOT YOUR CLONE

I've been misunderstood
more often than the meaning of ironic,
have enough scars to fill each line of a sonnet
with ten syllables of anguish,
as the consequences languish
in unexpected hidey-holes.

I've scored own goals, it's true,
but few were scored unaided
by the prejudice of those who decided
I was different to them
because they misjudged the angles
from which I came
and got their undergarments tangled
as they exclaimed disgust at what I said.

I want to put the past to bed,
start afresh and tell you where I stand,
pull together all the strands
to present the world with an image,
more photograph than painting,
unsullied by agendas and untruths
of the artists on both sides.

I am no saint. I never said I was.
If I decide to be a bastard
it's always in retaliation.
I've been pretty good at it
when I've had to be,
but fundamentally, that's not me.

My background is at once well known
and barely known at all.
There are facts that I have told,
some others that I still withhold
because I've been betrayed
by those I trusted in the past
and doubt I'll ever cast a net
in the sea of total trust again.

To have a loved one turn into a mirror
reflecting past torment, magnified
to everyone who wants to see it,
is as hurtful as the pain they share stripped bare.

This is where I've come from.
Some don't care to ask
but condemn me for rough edges
and will never listen to pledges of support
for their particular cause,
because I'm not them, of course.

I was raised to see things differently
and it's never easy breaking free
of how your life was shaped
and emerging with some dignity.

I lack the grace to be
a perfect member of the human race
but I'm not into discrimination.
I try not to be blinkered.
I am not in any way extremist
except in the eyes of right-wing thinkers.

I don't agree with anyone about everything
(not even Jeremy Corbyn),
and everyone has the right to what they think.
It's not for me to silence them.
Even if I could, why should I?
If they start spouting hatred, yes.
For thinking differently to me? No. Never!

But of course it takes its toll
and I would have to be a fool
not to learn some lessons from it all.

In my comedy, I've changed my style –
I no longer do work with a twist at the end
if it's going to send those out to be offended

into such judgemental fits of bile
that they can't contain self-righteous rage
for long enough to hear the final line,
the last word on the page
which puts a dent in their assumptions.

If I'm in character, I'm careful to make it clear,
though I realise that some will never be endeared
if they set out with the mindset of rejection.

When I wrote about an atheist who died –
obviously not me, as I'm still alive –
he found out he was wrong.
All his fantasies went through his head
as he reached the gates of Heaven –
even those of women, as a heterosexual male.

This to some was beyond the pale
and to them this fictitious man
will always be in Heaven
because they heckled and condemned
before I reached the end
where the God he got to meet
was female and damned well
cast the sexist bastard into Hell.

Pity they missed that bit, really.

There was that anti-homophobia piece
which got me branded homophobic
because I wrote it with a comic twist.
My gay friends who heard it found it fine
but someone unleashed the hounds of Hell
before they tried to understand the punchline.

So now I am resigned to being more transparent
because it is apparent that some
will never get the joke
if it doesn't have a handbook.

So here is the index, chapter by chapter,
for my ideal ever after.

True integration.
One people, one nation.
Love and peace.
Equality.
Race doesn't matter, nor does gender.
Acceptance is better than
Needless rejection.
Coming together, we can achieve
Everything in which we believe.

Now that is an acrostic spelling out tolerance.

So accept me for what I am
and what I'm not.
Shake my hand and be happy
that, although I'm not your clone,
you will never have to fight alone.

AN AS YET UNTITLED BIT OF 4AM CAN'T SLEEP MADNESS (YES, THAT IS NOW THE TITLE)

Saturday morning.
My thoughts a mess
as I tried to guess the best scenario
of how the day would play.
I tried to say I knew the way
that everything would be OK
but was talking shit
with no one listening anyway.

My demeanour was fifty shades of grey,
but not in that badly written kinky kind of way.
No. Grey as in dullard, uninteresting,
where the greatest thing about me
is I make a smashing pot of tea.
But I drink it all myself, of course,
because an hour with me is the road to insanity,
bored out your skull and yelling profanities,
staggering and dazed
like a wasp smashing brains
against double-glazed panes
in a desperate effort to flee.

Saturday afternoon.
No clue what to do,
no canny plan,
no direction and, upon reflection,
no hope of being a popular man.

So I stole a camper van,
had this idea to drive to Ikea,
ditch tedious banality
and buy a Swedish personality
to put together when I got it back
to my rather less than immaculate flat
which stank of cat piss and cannabis.

I'm not a fan of this pre-prepared cack
cheap crap flat pack bought by sad saps
who think it good form to conform
to a boring norm
like Norman and Norma Normal
or the Swedish-born nerds
Bjorn and Ljorna Njormalberg.

But it's what people like
and I need to be liked,
so I prepared to reveal the brilliant light
of the shiny new me
with the ready-made personality,
let everyone see how good I can be
with the flaws tucked away
behind doors and ignored.

But it didn't quite go as expected.
When the finished product was inspected
there were a few loose screws
and some bits that refused
to fit anywhere,
misfits like size twelve feet
in size seven shoes,
and soon I made the local news
as the guy who was Bjorn to lose.
The desperate Dan who failed as a man,
found guilty of stealing a camper van.

THE FUTURE'S BRIGHT...

There's a man-child in the White House,
an unbalanced shitehouse
with his finger on the button
of mutually assured destruction,
a prat with an orange complexion
who upon closer inspection
is not mutton dressed as lamb
but a fucking bellend of a man,
a prick dressed as a prick
with hair like melted marzipan
and the mentality of an orang-utan.

He is the real Donald Trump,
the result of a creator taking a dump,
and when he gets the hump he tweets
like a child denied his favourite sweets,
threatening, ranting, baiting, bleating,
covfefe is a word he's preaching.

The man's so orange it takes the pith.
He's a dollop of citrus-scented shit.
As a kid he couldn't see the humour
in always being called *Satsuma*.
Oh yes, we laugh.
A figure of fun,
the jokes have been done to death.

But has it stopped being funny yet?
When does it stop being funny?

When he denies climate change,
withdraws from accords?
Leaves a dying world untreated
as it gasps for breath
because he has the best of what is left
but still wants more?
This has already happened,
so what are we laughing for?

Does it stop being funny
when the dick that takes the gun to school
is in a position to do so
because of the power of fools like Trump
who resist gun control
not out of ideology
but for cold hard cash –
and those dead children could still be alive
if not for the bribes?
That's what happens when morals and money clash.

Does it stop being funny
when his childish belligerence
takes us closer to nuclear holocaust
than we've been for fifty years or more?
When a hissy fit edges us
that bit nearer incineration,
the end of nations?
You know this is happening, of course.

Or does it stop being funny
only when he's impeached or dead
and all the women he's molested
feel safe to go ahead
with tales of abuse,
of a maniac on the loose
who had too much power to accuse?

It's not sounding so funny now.
Maybe, somehow,
it stopped being funny
before we laughed at all.
We're like doomed people
with a terminal illness –
petrified, powerless –
nowhere to hide from the consequence,
just waiting for the worst to come,

and all we can do is accept our fate,
laugh in its face,
call its bluff and hope for a cure
before it's too late for all of us.

SIX

They served the time for someone else.
Named and blamed, framed and shamed
to douse the flames of outrage.

It was all too easy.
A game for those with a job to do
but no concrete clues,
nothing to lose in their reckless desire
that someone had to pay the dues.

Wrong place, wrong time, wrong nationality.
Who cares about the lives of family men
if their profiles scream guilty
when the twisting of reality
brands them and robs them of their liberty?

No smoke without fire,
a belief so widely held
by those who never choked
on manufactured fumes,
never felt the pain of injustice
from the inside of a prison cell.

And, of course, there are certain crimes
so heinous as to ensure
that once found guilty
there is more to endure than mental anguish.
Vengeance has its own language
centred around the physical.

When the truth is revealed
the breaks and bruises may be healed
but the greatest pain remains, invisible.
Indivisible from the victim.

So when the verdict's quashed
they're free to go.

Free to be abused
by those who refuse to adjust their views,
because they saw the fire,
the flames that never existed
beyond ham-fisted policing
and a diet of fabrication
fed to an angry nation.

Free –
as free as birds with broken wings,
the families of the victims
who are locked in ruthlessly remorseless grief
because they're never going to know the truth.

Free to find that compensation
cannot buy back the past they lost,
erase the lies that cost
the best part of their lives,
or take the hatred out of people's eyes.
Their innocence forever scrutinised
as the names of real barbarians
may never be publicised.

NO GREATER GOOD

There is no greater good
than standing your ground
and in the face of provocation
not propounding violence
out of sheer retaliation.
The power of choice is strong
and we can still control our destiny
with a propensity to hold on to
the standards we hold dear,
that our grandparents fought for
in a distant instance of the horrors of war.

Fight fire with fire only when the need is dire
and when it is then give no quarter,
but the better option is usually water.
The rise of the extreme right
is a symptom of a failed system,
a mass of people let down, disappointed,
lives broken and disjointed,
and we have to stop those who will exploit it,
we have to resist,
but brains beat bullets in the end
and although we can't pretend
this is an easy route,
what is beyond dispute
is that tit for tat becomes a trend,
a vicious circle of suffering and death,
grief and despair,
and the bad guys want to take us there.

The world stands on the brink of war
and, as before, defeat of fascism –
and all fanaticism – is a cause worth dying for,
but only as a last resort.

No one ever wins, despite such claims.
An ideology may be tamed
(to rise again another time)

but that list of names grows ever longer –
loved ones forever gone,
memories rendered worthless
by the madness of humankind.
Faces never again to be seen,
voices to never again be heard
except in the cold lies of technology.
Past times, preserved but out of reach,
the ultimate cruelty of deceit,
a final kick-in-the-teeth defeat.
Let's honour the dead by making peace.

A BETTER WORLD

There can be a better world,
where the banner of fairness is unfurled
and love is much more prevalent.
Where colour is an unimportant fact,
not a sign of different factions,
and religion is irrelevant –
race doesn't matter anymore.
Gender is never a bar,
and the scar of homophobia is healed
when we end our inaction,
neutralise the fear that the privileged yield
as a subtle shield against progressive change
and get the hatred of past prejudice repealed,
revealed as a con trick of the age.

This world isn't perfect.
It never can be if it houses humans,
as humans are destructive,
but most people can be trusted to be decent
if the opportunity is there
and those who can't should be aware
of the coming change of season.

A better world exists.
I dream about it in my bed,
wake up with it spinning in my head
and talk wherever words can be heard and said.

It's in your minds too.
We need to start anew,
find another way to do
the running of the world.
And the only thing preventing it is us.

If it can be dreamed and can be thought
then history has taught us that it can be done.
Good is easier than evil once it has begun.
The start just takes imagination.

Greed only wins when apathy lets it.
Elitism will fall when everyone gets this.
So spread the word.
The belief that we can't change things is absurd,
drilled into us by those who have the tools,
who take us for fools and serve themselves,
keep our hopes stacked on the shelves of selfishness,
hide our pride under piles of lies
and tell us only they are wise enough to wield power.
Their propaganda is another flammable tower,
but when this one burns, no innocents die.

Our time is coming. Getting closer by the hour.
The poor have been neglected,
their homes left ruined and derelict,
children uneducated and dejected,
their pleas rejected,
as the victim is depicted as the cause.

We want what can't be done, they say.
There is no magic money tree, they say,
but they pay the DUP
to help them cling to their positions.
And we are sickened.

The NHS wasn't possible.
Women's suffrage wasn't possible.
A black US president wasn't possible.
Same-sex marriage wasn't possible.
But each impossibility happened somehow
when the will of the people made it so.

We still have many miles to go.
But the lesson we must learn
is never to accept it
when the powers that be say no.

When they say it can't be done,
it often means they're on the run.

NEARLY HOME?

This early August evening,
as the light begins to fade
to match my shade of mood,
I look around.
Half a mile from what I now call home
it strikes me, as it often does,
how out of place I am.

This scene's so far removed
from what I know,
in more than mere miles –
on nights like these it's another world
somewhere to aspire to
if you are hoodwinked
into thinking that material worth
is the only reason for our birth.

Driveways littered with Mercs and Beamers
with number plates screaming
how much their owners have to waste.
Large detached houses
encasing cold detached people
who have everything desired by dreamers
from the streets where I grew up.

Is this enough?
Are they happy where they dwell?
They will point to their wares
and insist they're doing well.
But what's the point of all the stress,
the drive to this apparent success,
if there's no one there for them to tell?

Net financial worth is not where it all ends.
That is greed and grand delusion.
I'd rather be on a council estate with friends
than a country estate which tends
to snobbery and exclusion.
And as for being somewhere in between,
I'm always looking back to where I've been.

THE ART OF LOVING (SOMEONE WHO LIKES YOU)

Don't ever stop loving someone
because they merely like you.
Just do it differently.

The world hasn't stopped turning –
they may not be returning
the feelings that engulf you
at the very mention of their name,
but they are still the same person,
a wonderful light that illuminates life
whenever they are around.

Respect the distance
but help them when you can.
Be there for them
when they need someone,
a friend to the end
because you know they're worth it,
that they deserve it
just for being who they are.

Don't pretend they'll ever love you back.

Real love is unconditional, unselfish.
To have them in your life at all
may be the best that you can really hope for.
Let that be enough.
Don't lose that gift if you can help it.

THE THIEF AND THE SUITCASE

Fuck! Fuck! Fuck!
This is typical of my luck.
Gliding with grace,
I stole a case from the luggage rack,
got off the train
and took it back to my place,
eager to see what I had gained
from under the nose of a careless twit
too pissed or stoned to notice,
pathetic prat who looked away
and let me take it, gratis.

So what did I get for my hard work,
the risk of taking someone else's things?

Dirty pants and sweaty socks,
cheap Asda clothes
that would only fit a tall fat bastard
with the dress sense of
Jeremy Corbyn or Michael Foot,
and some pretty poncey poetry books.

I had to take a second look!
It seems he was more likely
to waste his money on Shakespeare or Byron
than buy decent clothes or invest in an iron.

(OK, the books were by Blackwell and Kegode,
but you'll understand, if you know me,
that I haven't heard of them.
My schooldays turned me right off poetry.)

Now I'm a scumbag with nothing below me
and I act as if society owes me.

THIS IS THE SUITCASE SPEAKING!
What did you expect?
You saw the state of me.
Was that not a clue?
Twenty years old, held together with glue?
Did you think I carried diamonds and rubies?

My owner is a fat twat
with very long arms and preposterous man boobs.
The clothes are no good to you.
Throw them away – they cost peanuts anyway.
The boxer shorts are dirty, unhygienic,
and be wary of the skid mark
if you haven't already seen it.

You're a worthless, petty crook,
but look, here's some advice…
Ditch the rest, but read the books.
Read them. Digest the decency
in the words you stole so recently.
Let them change your life,
lead you to the light,
See the power of poetry
to make things feel right.

BAH, HUMBUG

I remember the date.
October the eighth.
A person who hates me approached
with a card in his hands
and a smile on his face.

I hadn't seen him smile
since I broke my wrist,
and he wouldn't aspire to waste his piss
to put out the fire if I combusted,
but would just stand and admire
and maybe sell tickets
if he thought he could do it
without being busted.

So what was the occasion,
the reason for evasion
of his usual brazen animosity?

Oh yes!

The annual generosity –
a fucking piece of cardboard
with a picture of Jesus
and a rhyme sure to please us.
(if we're eight years old
and happy to believe any shit we're told
by those who peddle capitalist wheezes).

Just five days into the twelve weeks of Christmas
(it used to be days, but this was extended
by the ultra-religious who never pretended
their god was anything other than money and greed
and the gullible wankers all followed their lead.)

So back to that October day,
the gift of the cardboard

he hoped I would copy
so it could go with his hoard
to prove popularity,
how people liked his fake jocularity
and great personality.

Well, fuck the feckless non-entity;
he won't be getting one from me!
What is with this hypocrisy?

Stuffing our faces with once-a-year treats
that we don't even like
but tradition dictates we have to buy.

Getting into debt,
being reckless and wasteful
for self-centred people
who are not even grateful
and then get upset because
someone else got more than them,
and say you are mean and thoroughly hateful?

Well, bollocks to it all –
you can keep your Messiah and Santa Claus,
wear your reindeer sweaters
and party with people no better than rats
who with no pause for thought
would put knives in your back,

embrace all the bullshit
for the season's goodwill.
Then wipe away tears
with your credit card bill.

HAPPY CHRISTMAS!!

REGRETS

The mild air belies the time of year
but it's early, and it's dark.
No need for gloves or scarves
as I saunter through the park
towards the last home
from the small part of your life
spent in this town
before departing to where we all called home,
the place I always knew you would return to
but expected it to be much later.

I'm proud of who you have become,
fulfilling all your cherished plans
despite my absent guiding hand.
You're grown up and you've blossomed,
with achievements which to me were dreams.
I never dreamt that I could do these things
but hoped this was what your life would bring,
despite it all.

Yet as I walk towards your old front door,
illuminated with Christmas lights
and the promise of Santa Claus,
even knowing what a star you are
as an adult going far,
tonight my conscience has no respite.

It hurts me how I failed you,
how she failed you,
how we failed you
and how we only ever get one shot.
How points scored in a petty war
became all you saw us living for
as we tore your life apart,
aimed to break each other's hearts
but just broke yours.
Time has moved on –

it always has and always will,
but the bitterest pill is memory,
the symptoms of an overdose
a tearstained face and the fear
that you will never feel close,
that you'll just go through the motions
because you feel a duty,
and the beauty of togetherness
was lost forever
when we had one precious, priceless chance
but failed to deliver.

DETERRENT

So this is how it works.
We are kept grounded by the force of gravity,
then crushed by the depravity of a world
where the greed of those with more than they need
compounds the misery of those we cannot feed.

We support a London arms fair
propagating death and despair,
supply both sides in unending wars
where we care not what they're fighting for
as long as they keep coming back for more

and we can look away from the screen
when children scream at the consequence
of what we've done,
then share their image on social media
to demonstrate our strong compassion

before we switch off monitors, turn pages
and the war gets ignored as it rages
and we don't see its victims,
scarred people of all ages
from the old and infirm to tiny babies.

Spending more than we can afford
on nuclear weapons we daren't deploy,
we then destroy all hopes of peace
by peddling a conventional cache
as, unabashed, we have the nerve to decide

to play roulette with people's lives,
and can't care for the elderly
with the dignity they deserve
in a system that's in meltdown
because of all the cutbacks.

Meanwhile we believe the crap
from bloated top-table diners
who enable this to happen
and do everything to silence those
who know how things could change.

Wrapped in a blanket of 'I'm alright, Jack',
we swallow propaganda. There is no turning back.
Those who campaign for a better world
are idealists, unrealistic in their expectations.
We must support nations fighting other nations

and other nations returning fire.
The resulting mire makes the world go round,
so cash abounds for the lucky few
as Jew kills Arab and Arab kills Jew
and murderous warlords do what they do.

There is no trickle-down effect
but they select their words so carefully
so we don't dare to be dismissive.
We're not dying. We're not starving.
The homeless stats may be alarming

but it has to be like this, it's not abhorrent.
Our way of living is secure
as long as we throw the lifeline
of the sick and the poor
at a multi-billion-pound deterrent.

NOISE

There are voices all around me.
Strangers, friends, internal sounds,
vipers and snipers who are really proud
to be an undercover enemy
with a mask of respectability,
a cacophony of messages
demanding to be heard,
trying to claim monopoly
of my attention,
so many words, each with their own intention.

Today the ones that make most noise
are the ones that sound annoyed,
the ones with hatred buoyed by lies
which avoid the facts to make a point.
Outsized weapons claiming centre ground
combine in a cruel joint venture
with insecurity and doubt
to out me as something somehow seedy,
someone to talk about in forks,
with a greedy malice in their thoughts.

Friendly noises are rendered silent
by the violence of insinuation
as my mind reacts to provocation,
closing down all roads to relaxation
or any form of peace.

Today, aggression comes out on top
and won't release the spoils it somehow got.
Tomorrow may be different, who knows?
I may be more composed.
But for now I fight the turmoil
which fills me, which kills me as it grows.

NOT RIGHT

I know… I should be happy,
and I am.
But I'm not.
Well, I dunno, you know?

It makes no sense to you?
You think it does to me?

Everything's good, but it's not right.

Yes, They're real tears…

It's true I've lots of friends.
and earn decent money.
So what do I do, pretend?
Say there's not a part of me
spoiling to tear it all apart,
bring me crashing down
to where I was before,
to take me right back to the start?

I don't *know* why!
Maybe I don't deserve what I've got.
Of *course* I can't allow it to.
What do you suggest for the best?
I put these feelings in a box
and burn them?

Don't you think I would if I could,
that I hate this silent torture,
the void I feel but can't locate?

I know you're trying to be a mate,
but it doesn't help. Not at this minute.
Come back when it's finished,
when I can appreciate it all again
and I'll apologise.

But now I'll hide my eyes
behind dark glasses if I must
until the moment passes.
I don't know when.
It's just…

SWEET

It seemed like a good idea at the time,
so I went for it with no fear in my mind.
Sweetness always wins in the end –
so I can't even begin to pretend
it didn't come as a bit of a shock.

'Fuck off, you cock.'
What?
'Fuck off, you cock.'

That's not very nice!
It's bad enough once, let alone twice.

'You stink.'
I couldn't help thinking this was just a bad dream,
that I would wake up
relieved to find it's not real.

'Have you got a bargepole?
I still wouldn't touch you, you arrogant arsehole.'

Jesus Christ, OK. I get the message.
You don't, erm, find me all that impressive,
but this is a little bit over-the-top.
I thought you were really nice,
not the nasty, sour, aggressive type.

'BO! Halitosis! Probably chlamydia!
Now get stuffed. I just want rid o' ya.
I've got no time for boring old farts!'

That's the last time I buy a packet of Love Hearts.

IMPARTIAL

This is the six o'clock news
with the impartiality of British TV.

The top story tonight.

The rich young couple who recently wed,
not at all at your expense,
have said they feel very blessed
to have such wide support
(though not in any way financial, of course)
and will soon gift us some further delight
as the breeding programme takes its course.
All very good for the tourist trade,
so lots of sterling will be made.
In other news, Brexit Brexit Brexit Brexit,
blah blah blah blah blah.

Will of the people, financial benefit,
windfall for the NHS,
Boris, Jacob, blah blah blah blah,
no vested interests detected so far.

Theresa's very perplexed
by this issue so divisive
but old Jeremy's not exactly decisive.
His party is particularly weak
in the impartial view
of our expert editorial team
who are all well paid for their incisive insight
(particularly the men, it seems).

Our political correspondent
drops us all a stern reminder
that Corbyn's a terrorist sympathiser,
a former Soviet conniver
and, in all probability, a drunk driver –

but in the interests of balance
he keeps his allotment tidy
and has probably given up spying
as old men need life simplifying.

In the Middle East
some unarmed protestors were massacred this week
near the border with their stolen land.
They probably deserved it,
as the mighty military machine was spooked
by the noise made by this motley band
and opened fire, they claim unplanned,
in understandable self-defence.

President Trump refused to enter conversations
or devise a plan with other nations
to address the human rights violations,
but tweeted his congratulations.
Which was great.

Justified mass killing is not new to them
but when the US recognises Jerusalem
as their capital
that is a gesture to cap it all.

Meanwhile the loony left
entered the debate
with antisemitism aimed at the besieged state,
and Hope Not Hate reversed their roles
like typical brainless commie trolls,
claiming unarmed civilians weren't a threat.
They've never failed to say this yet,
lest we should ever forget their pet agenda,
when spouting blatant propaganda.

In other news
a celebrity showed some flesh
in her specially designed expensive dress
for some or other awards,

England got a goalless draw,
and, oh yeah, homelessness, poverty, famine, war,
Syria, Yemen.
Mentally ill white man mows down and kills eleven.
Brexit Brexit, David Davis
unemployment, labour savings.
Whatever.
Now here's a pretty woman with the weather.

NOTHING IS REAL

So here I am,
stretching my fingers like elastic
to reach the glory there before me,
teasing like a misconception,
a stack of invisible gold
infused with contentment
the like of which was sold
to chase the false perceptions.

Its fragrance fills my nostrils,
unique in its blend of hope and sweetness,
the completeness of its power
hooking me like opiates,
my system defenceless to its lure,
my dependence inappropriate,
disproportionate to probability
but oh, so typical of me.

I've always wanted to believe,
been gullible in the face of schemes
designed to draw me in.
So I keep on reaching
in the certain knowledge it is there,
reachable and real,
genuine in its appeal.

The day will come when it doesn't drift away
and it will fit me perfectly.
I'm absolutely certain it's not a game,
an illusion for which to aim
to be revealed as nothing different,
just another dose of the same old thing,
another sting behind the mask of better days.

So I keep on clinging to the promise,
the desire that is always just too distant
but so insistent of its honesty.

I chase the dream,
convince myself that dreams don't lie,
they merely make suggestions –
then reality gets in the way,
I miss the chance or fuck it up –

But one day, just once,
it will all click into place,
stick around and leave no trace
of another what-might-have-been.

It helps me cope to keep on thinking
that nothing is real except for hope,
that reward is sealed in an envelope
waiting to be opened.

This gift may not exist
but it's hard to resist
the pull of a pact with chance,
a change of circumstance
just waiting in the wings.
An ounce of truth
to counter the deceit of everything.

IF...

If I were your hot water bottle
I'd burst as you were dozing off.
I would become a Bolshevik
if I thought you were a Romanov.

If bacon is a killer
then I will cook you breakfast.
If I see much more of you
I'll earn a prison sentence.

If you were God, I'd go to Hell.
I would!
If you were Satan, I'd be really good.
If you were specs, I'd rather squint.
I'd be pneumonia were you Gustav Klimt.

But you're the boss and I need the money.
So my nose is brown
and your jokes are funny.

NIGHT AND DAY

Can we ever be just friends?
Now the light of our day has given way
to the darkness of its end,
can dawn bring a new dimension
or will the tension kill it dead,
changed landscapes fill our heads
with resentment or regrets?

When the night's been spent in restlessness
it must be worth a shot.
We've only got one life;
it's packed with personal regret
and pointless strife.
Let's not forget the warmth
we felt together.

OK, it couldn't last forever
and the heartbreak of the final hours
devoured the memory of the morning.
I had ignored the warnings
as sweetness turned to sour,
as air polluted and power shifted
from our feelings as we drifted.

Now we begin another day,
another chapter in our ever after,
and I'm happy that you're there,
not wanting to share a lifetime
but still to know and care, both aware
that you don't always have to be lovers
to really love each other.

WHAT'S YOUR EMERGENCY? (2020)

Hi. My name is Sir Richard Branson.
You have reached the Virgin Emergency 999 service.
Calls are charged at £1 per minute
but please don't use mobiles (unless it's Virgin)
because that will cost considerably more
and I won't get to keep it all.

We need to know the nature of your emergency.
If you need an ambulance,
I don't rate your chance
and you probably can't afford the treatment anyway.
But if all other hope has gone, press one.
For the fire service, press two.
I'm sure someone will get to you.
For police, press three.
There won't be any bobbies free,
but thanks to me you can buy private security
for a modest fee.

If you are just another clown
claiming you have a virgin emergency,
please end this call and have a wank
as a matter of urgency,
or consider joining our dating service
at www.virginonthedesperate.com
or press star to be transferred to this separate con
on 686868. That's as close as you'll get, mate.

You pressed one for ambulance. Is this correct?
Please say no or yes.

I'm sorry. I didn't understand what you said.
Please try again.

You have asked for an ambulance.

We are sorry to announce
that the Virgin ambulance service in your area
has been cancelled.

This is due to a lack of trained paramedics
willing to work for less than they'd get
working at Lidl or at Ladbrokes taking bets.
There is a replacement bus service.
Do you wish to continue?

May we take this opportunity
to thank you for calling
the Virgin emergency 999 hotline?
We're sure with us things will be fine.
Before we tell you where the bus stops
it's important to know that if you have Sky TV
your first consultation will only be free
if you switch to Virgin Media.

Do you wish to continue?

I'm sorry. I didn't understand your reply.
Please speak clearly or be left to die.

It sounded like you said 'aaahhhhh'.

Please consider Virgin funeral care.
We offer the best burials anywhere.

COLIN

Inspired by Alphabet Spaghetti by Stephen Thomas.

Colin can calculate conundrums,
cleverly crushing challenges,
cucumber-cool, confidence creeping ceaselessly.

Colin can charm complete clans,
cheerily, cunningly creating control .

Clive calls Colin 'Cumstain'.
Callous Colin chuckles,
crafting Clive's comeuppance,
countering childish catcalling creatively,
contemptuously.

Cock!

ARSON

If you see or smell the fire
don't be disconcerted
or call the fire brigade.
This is no emergency.
Instead, join me
in dancing round the edges,
bring the fuel and fan the flames.
It took a lot of courage
to strike the match
and watch the blaze take hold.

I want this out the way,
this comfort zone in which I alone
could sense the closing in of walls.
I need more space in which to stretch
and can't forget the thoughts
that were going through my head,
the nights I couldn't sleep,
the knowledge of the wasted chances,
my own responsibility
for my circumstances.

Feel the heat. Let it burn
until I have no possible return.

BILL

Bill had nothing until that fateful night.
Picked up butts in search of a smoke,
went to the foodbank
but would still laugh and joke
about how one day he would take flight,
make a fortune and see his mates right.

Then he 'found a tenner in the street'
(still swears to this day he didn't nick it
even though I was a tenner light),
bought himself some fish and chips
and spent the rest on a lottery ticket.

EuroMillions multi-rollover week
is always appealing when your life is so bleak
you steal a copy of the *Mail* or the *Sun*
simply to wipe your bum,
the only highlight when you're up shit creek.

Well, fuck me with a stump from the cricket –
he only went and bloody won it.
Found himself on an easier wicket
and started smashing old friendships for six
as he decided what to do with it.

Mega money changes things,
corrupts the mind,
and Bill changed more than most,
would boast he was more refined
as his purpose in life was redefined.
That's what he liked to think.

If being refined is buying posh cutlery,
getting gardeners, cooks and butlers in,
wiping your arse on real currency,
dressing like an Eton twat in a top hat and cravat,
then he made it, didn't he?

He took lessons to learn to speak like the Queen,
says, 'Awfully sad,' and, 'Orf with his head.'
But sometimes when out with the local hunt
he forgets himself and says *fuck* and *cunt*
to the fucking cunts.

He plays polo and croquet but is a football fan
and remembers his time on the terraces.
He wears a tux to the local pub
but the coarseness is all he inherited.

His political discourse is quite absorbing,
he claims admiration for Jeremy Corbyn,
but when the time comes he votes for the Tories
because he'll never be one of us again.

He drives a Bentley but goes on the bus
to visit his mum on the council estate
because the plebs he grew up with
drive battered old bangers
and burnt his Ferrari to win the debate.

He is the man between two stools –
too clever in his head for working-class fools,
too rough and ready for snobs and toffs
who fob him off as a commoner
who eats from a trough.

He got lucky, grew too big for his boots,
got the cash but not the class,
tried to be flash, denied his roots
and ended up a pseudo-upper-class twat.

There's no bigger nob than a working-class snob
who will never do it proper.
So get your head from up your arse
and rehouse your mum, you tosser.

BLAME

You think you know what happened
by the answers to your questions.
Except they were only fractions of the whole,
views skewed by stories told,
perceptions loaded
by the one half that you interviewed.

Like flipping a coin and getting tails.
You could learn the details from someone else,
get a totally different thread,
toss again and come up heads.
The ship has sailed, firm evidence lost
and the best chance you have got
is to put away the coin and roll a die.

Then roll again and keep on rolling,
tally the score, watch it unfolding
and as the average approaches pi
accept you may be somewhere near right.
Each party to the truth
holds their own warped versions dear.
It's what we as humans do.

How often do we think
to add the two contrasting tales
and divide the sum by two?

HOLDING ON

It pays to be aware and listen for the signs,
feel the change in pressure as your life is realigned,
accept that often people change their minds,
what once felt right is left behind
and no one alive knows how to press rewind.

Sometimes, clinging to something you know is dead
can effectively kill you too,
eat you from the inside out
as your dignity struggles to survive
until eventually it dies
and you have nowhere left to hide.

In reality the demise may well be no one's fault.
Circumstances can build walls, change borders
like some unstoppable force,
and trying to halt them is the human thing to do.
Resistance to change is as natural to the mind
as that change is to the wider world.

Letting go of what you had
is the hardest thing of all,
the greatest fall from grace
that most of us can ever face,
even when it's hurting and there is no trace
of the joy it used to bring,
just day after day of stolen dreams
as your wished-for schemes fall apart at the seams.

You know – at least subconsciously –
that a fracture's going to hurt,
but not as much as the cancer
that has got you in its grip.
If you find the courage to break away
it feels like defeat, like life is incomplete
and will never be the same.
And it won't.

Because you've released the source of pain,
not the good times which were never coming back again.
The gloom will suffocate your sense of worth
as day by day the hurt grows worse.
Until, suddenly. A spark, a flame…

IT'S OVER

It's time for me to retire from professional boxing.
There was always something beautifully relaxing
about punching people to the point of coma,
picking them up off the canvas,
them not knowing if they're in Brum or Kansas –
another good day's work hurting people,
being the macho manly type
who always won the fight
and loving my fans as much
as they loved my rippling muscles.
I mean. Look at those muscles!

But the hustle and bustle of the fight game
is in the past, I'm afraid to say.
Yes, it's still a thrill to half-kill someone
with a neat right hook
and be eulogised in books about the noble art.

But I've started getting hit myself
and I nearly fucking shit myself
when I felt how much it hurt,
and I'm certain now's the time to stop.

The fact is my pretty-boy looks
are still intact
and with my fine physique
and handsome face
there's no disgrace in modelling.

For some, the future's bleak
when the fighting's done,
but not for me.
I'm lucky I'm so beautiful
and can afford cosmetic surgery
when my face begins to crack.

But of course there is no urgency,
as you can see,
and when I'm old and have no money
I can go on I'm a Celebrity
before the one last desperate comeback.

INNOCENCE

There are times when words won't do,
when no poem or song can cut through
the thickness of the suffering caused
by the sickness of a few.

Now is such a time.
We can do our best to spread some love,
express our horror at a crime.
But the clocks can't be turned back

to when those kids were innocent,
when they believed all that mattered
was the music, the thrill of a concert,
a night of magic in a vibrant city.

Right now, words are aspirin fighting cancer,
a piece of paper to halt a storm.
Not remotely like a probable answer
to all the killing still to come.

But they're all we have,
and in the longer term
could well be the ingredient we need
to turn the tides of hate-filled seas.

However, bear in mind that some are toxic.
Sort the mushrooms from the toadstools –
because any fool can preach deceit and poison.
Examination is the key.

Hatred breeds hatred, death multiplies its naked truth.
'Our' kids, 'their' kids are all the same.
Innocent of bullshit until indoctrinated.
And any child's killing is insane.

THE TOWER

Injustice drips unnoticed to all but victims.
Drip… drip… drip. Not for minutes, or hours or days,
but years flowing into decades,
callous ignorance and carelessness
propped up by vested interests and propaganda
slowly filling to overflowing
the tolerance which keeps it all held in.

We all know the cause of this horrific scene.
To be obscene enough to demonise the innocent,
those caught up in the terror,
publish photos under phoney headlines
is more than just a foolish error.
It is a conscious effort to increase tensions
and turn the people away from truth.
But dear *Daily Mail*, this time you've failed.

This was a result of greed
in a system where those in need
are not worth the investment,
not worth the effort.
They had their pleas ignored
and the cause of death
was underscored by negligence.

Saving money, cutting corners,
ignoring warnings in reports
is like an act of war against the poor,
telling them their lives are worthless
to the landlords and the state.
In a city of such riches,
such disregard of life and rights
is nothing short of criminal.
And we're demanding justice.

When the Prime Minister can't lower herself
to speak to people full of grief,

such arrogance is beyond belief.
The time has come to change the game.

That silent drip drip drip
becomes the noisy tick tick tick
of a time bomb being primed.

If you think the plebs don't matter,
it's time to make you change your mind.

TECHNIQUE

There has to be a metaphor
to turn this bucket of rotting fish
into meaningful art.
But fuck it, I can't think of one.
Part of me says poetic people persist in placing
far too much emphasis on technique,
all meaning obliterated as words are alliterated,
assonance arrogantly blasted out
by people with no confidence in consonance,
producing puerile nonsense verse.

So my work will sit unloved
like Donald Trump at a Women's Institute meal
in a Mexican restaurant
as the curse of worthless shite
haunts everything I write.
Proper poetry perplexes me,
doggerel relaxes me, sets me free
and the crown of clueless clown
is my property.
Just don't ask me to explain simile.
It's like a billow of smoke
drifting down a chimney.

TEMPTATION

I only sat down to watch the match,
the clash of the Titans at the Etihad,
billionaires v. millionaires,
continental, debonair,
playing with brilliance and flair.

And yes, I hate the way the game betrays its past,
bestowing riches for kicking a ball,
how Rupert Murdoch screwed us all
so the game is out of reach for many fans.
But I'm a little bit of a twat
and a hypocrite at that,
so I pay Sky subscriptions
and watch from the comfort of my flat
(and at least my team's near bankrupt
and totally crap).

This, though, is big. City v. Arsenal.
Football of the highest class
with commentary quite farcical
and pundits speaking out of their ass.

Nearly kick-off time, so one more round of adverts,
brewers and bookies looking for converts.
Supermarkets with dirt-cheap booze
to drown your sorrows when you lose –
but don't forget to drink responsibly,
there's a good chap and all that crap.

Then when you're sozzled and your mind's befuddled
don't forget to have a bet.

Four-two to City, with three headed goals, two sendings-off,
eight yellow cards and a penalty-box trip,
Wenger losing a fight with a zip?
We can quote you odds for that.
Then if there's a third sending-off,
have another bet to chase your loss.

But don't try being sensible
because winners are not acceptable
and losers are easy to spot.
They're the ones still allowed to bet,
the addicts that self-control forgot
who, once the fun stopped, couldn't stop.

Another glass? Don't mind if you do!
An Aguero hat trick now eleven to two,
with a free bet thrown in if you lose
(terms and conditions mean we often refuse).

But no! It's Premier League, don't forget.
I don't need a skinful or a stupid bet.
I won't regret it. You're missing the point.
It's a whole different ball game
when you're smoking a joint.

ALL THE SAME

Beneath the shiny surface
lurks a murky secret.
We stake our claims
in wanting change,
make a pledge but rarely keep it.
Most of us are too consumed,
at least in our subconscious,
by the bits that work for us.

It's presumed we tell the truth
when we proclaim our goals again
but we are pretenders
who secretly resist those aims
to suit selfish agendas.

We've all arrived from different places
and the challenges each person faces
are known only to them.
We are all quick to condemn
the other point of view as wrong,
somehow unworthy of attention.
It may not be intentional
but it's there in all of us.
We may sing the same song in principle,
but personal views are invincible
in the mindset of most people.

I am no different.
I'm firm in my beliefs
but they've shifted over time.
I'm not the person I was ten years ago
or even ten months ago
but I've still got a way to go
before I grow to be
the person I would wish,
and it's good that I know this.
I can work at the improvement,

the constant movement from
the past me to the person that I want to be.
I can't see what other people see
and if I could the revelation might set me free
from the ties that hold me back.
But this ability is something all humans lack
and I'm only human,
just one more member of a seething mass.

What I do long for is the day
when everyone has equality,
the same chances of a quality of life
regardless of who or what they are.

Even those with the same dream
have a whole wide spectrum of ideas
on how they can achieve it.
There are silent types and demagogues,
the political and the apathetic,
but the crucial thing is dialogue.
Without it grievance festers,
people grow to detest the allies
who then become the enemy
despite the core beliefs.

This will remain the same
until we learn to say,
'I hear you.'
And mean it.

Life is not a game.
We are chained to preconditioning
and we see life from a goldfish bowl
of selfish needs and jealousy
with age-old seeds of prejudice
in varying degrees.
The pity is, we just don't see it.

MUSIC

They say this music is sublime,
that the beauty of the world
is there to find in its hypnotic rhythm.

I've tried. I've tried so hard to hear it,
listened to detect the nuances of sound
combining to bring pleasure,
feel the joy of being alive,

but the highs seem to elude me
like tomorrow evades today,
a promise that is oh so close
though just too far away.

Yet still the music plays,
each semibreve makes me believe
it will leave me behind,
undeserving of its finer points
and its supposed divine simplicity,

never knowing what it was
that touched the souls of everyone
yet destroyed me with duplicity.

HOW TO BE LIKE ME

Let every nuance of your character be influenced
by the worst excesses of your parents,
even when they've long departed.
Cultivate the things they started,
grow a chip on your shoulder
that gets more bitter as you grow older.

Detach yourself from the world
when all the best times should unfurl,
then emerge with good intentions
submerged by bad decisions.

Be kind to those who will abuse it
then will have no time to lend an ear
when you could use it.

Let past events make deep incisions,
then leave revision of your goals too late,
not even open to debate,

Squander the one true gift you have
until it hates you,
then face a battle to win it back,
while all the time you feel trapped,
strapped in and ready for a ride to nowhere,

chasing each chink of light
until it explodes like dynamite,
scars your scars
and pins you firmly where you are,
not exactly living in the past,
more slowly dying in it,

choking on the toxic smoke
that clouds all hope.
This doesn't have to be,
but when most everyone you ever trusted

breathed betrayal
when everyone you've loved has failed you
(or maybe you failed them?)
it's easy then to fail yourself.

It takes strength to carry on
when all conclusions seem foregone,
forever entombed, no room for manoeuvre
in the depths of gloom.

But I'm stronger than I may appear,
so to be like me you keep on trying,
accept that these emotions can recur
when things go wrong,
then cry when you feel like crying.

You feel hurt more keenly than you should
but, however bad it's been,
however hard it's hit you,
you reach a time when life is good,
when at last you feel more understood
and you see all possibilities anew.

SCHOOL REPORT

Clive is noted on our files
as being a rather odd child.
He gives the impression
of a thug in wimp's clothing
with an obvious loathing of authority
but without the oomph to mount an insurrection –
or even get an erection
when anyone switched on would be aroused.

Personally I see no potential for him
to be anything other
than an inconsequential little squirt
who flirts with a colourless existence,
though there is an insistence among some teachers
that he could become a serial killer
or, even worse, a poet,
taking organs from his victims to sell
or writing sonnets and villanelles.
He is deeply unpopular
and highly unlikely ever to copulate,
which is probably a blessing
as the thought of any offspring from that thing
is quite depressing.

The biggest problem is he's ginger.
Now, don't shoot the messenger,
because I know that sounds discriminatory,
but I didn't create the laws of probability
and it is a fact that statistically
most people associate this affliction in males
with an addiction to sexual DIY,
a temper to make a stone statue cry
and a lifetime of unfortunate travails.

Some of this disposition are rumoured to be
a product of James Hewitt's bodily fluids,
though in this case, it's true, it's unlikely.

But this child could be heir to the throne
and, looking like that,
would still grow old and die alone.

With his caveman of a father,
the future's looking pretty stark.
He may as well flee to the safari park
and let the monkeys teach him how to wipe his arse,
because, judging by the smell, no one's taught him so far.

To sum up, he's ugly and smelly
with an oversized belly,
has the social skills of a hippopotamus
and lacks the drive to improve his status.
But I, as head teacher, couldn't care less
because as of this moment, I'm on a hiatus.

WORTHWHILE?

I write my best words in the darkest times
when I'm saddened by the headlines
or my life's design is not in line
with what my mind desires.

I'm told that's fine. That writing is a therapy
and it's better to be productive
than feeling sorry for myself.
That it's better for my health.

Yeah. For sure.
Like words let loose can cure the blues
when you've lost all you ever had to lose
and the future is a noose around your neck.

Well, here's a reality check. It doesn't help.
Nothing changes when it's on the page.
There's no rainbow to camouflage the pain.
They're just letters methodically arranged.

They make a sound to please the ear.
If I could rearrange them to soothe the heart
or lift me from this darkness
then that would be a start. But I can't.

When all you want is out of reach
and the past is a deserted beach
destroyed by massive oil slicks,
words won't ever do the trick.

If this is how I have to feel
to write worthwhile verse, then screw it.
I'd rather that I didn't do it.
I never even wanted to be a poet.

UNEASY

There's this eerie feeling in the air,
an uneasy peace, yet a sure sign
that this could be the end of time.
Maybe Trump has pressed the button
and I am dumped in a sort of in-between,
neither dead nor alive,
not knowing whether to laugh or cry,
live or die, not understanding why
I've got no WiFi.

I haven't been on Facebook since yesterday,
so I have no way of knowing
if the world continues unabated
or if a minister's been caught masturbating
over question time.
Don't know if a poetry snob
has called out Tempest over dodgy rhyme,
haven't seen if Kathy's cat still looks divine
or even if my writing has been plagiarised
(this is highly unlikely, I realise).

I miss my friends but can't go through the door,
go out, explore the beauty of the world.
It's dangerous out there
and I freely admit I'm fucking scared.
I need a new computer,
a new WiFi router
to deduce the current state of play.
Has Billy carried out his threat and gone away,
deactivated his account
because everyone is beastly,
or did the trick work neatly
and bring a thousand likes,
bring lots of smiley faces to the table
to make him more emojinally stable?

Are people still asking questions
not looking for answers
but outing those who would betray them
by having different views?
Have I been unfriended by just the one
or are they forming queues?

Facebook, I love you,
can't survive without you by my side.
You're like a best friend and a wife;
you fill my life with joy and strife
(not necessarily respectively, obviously).

Come back to me. I'm lonely.

CODEINE DREAMS

Outsized wasps at every turn –
winter-hardened swarms
swooping with a sting that burns,
causes agony with its toxins,
destroys the skin from the outside in,
bringing panic to the masses,
a morass of frantic fighting
to escape the flash of hatred
from insects as big as birds.

But it gets worse.

Those like me who don't get stung
are on the run and stunned to find
the world has wrung the changes,
old certainties are disarranged
as a new world order is in place,
diurnal multi-coloured bats, misshapen rats
and noises like I've never heard
fill the senses as a chill descends
upon my flesh.

I'm on a road I know, but anxiety grows
as people I once recognised
mutate before my eyes.
I hear a cry of 'People are dying.
People are dying.'

A frozen lake
that wasn't there last time I looked
begins to bubble,
spewing deathly poison into air.
The only hope is the huddle of people
gathered in the rubble of a steeple
offering solutions,
but their resolution is not enough.
'People are dying! People are dying!'
The voices drift away.
The world falls silent.

DREAMING

All I had were dreams –
tomorrows wrapped in some vague hope
to blunt the impact of today,
the only way to deal with pain,
goals undefined yet burning through reality,
escape routes from the insularity of youth,
tunnels only I could see,
uncharted, but the only way to prove my worth.

I clung to them as darkness marched
like well-armed raiders, merciless invaders
of a feeble conquered nation,
beseeching them to neutralise
the impact of being brutalised,

a form of resistance
that no one could detect or intercept
as it reflected light
on the wasteland strewn with rubble
from a past beset with troubles.

Liberation never comes without a fight.
There's no divine right to smile.
At times I lost all sight of aims
across the miles of my enemy's gains
and I struggled to reignite the flames.

But the dreams remained, sustained the remnants
of a dormant faith that things could change,
readied them for action
when the sense of resignation
began to fade,
when the longed-for opportunity came.
When one bid failed
they gave the strength to try again.

And again.

Because dreams don't always stay the same.

They're shapeshifting wizards
with the power to lead the way,
stay out of reach while making you believe.

I still do.

Each night I dream anew.

And wonder if you do too.

TRUTH

We are here to serve you.
Motivated by your needs,
our deeds inspired by your interests.
We are the good guys
who protect you from the lies
of the corrupt and self-obsessed,
do our best to guide you to the light,
to always do things right.

We have no agenda,
no need for propaganda,
just a simple aim to tell the truth,
to warn you of abuse of power
perpetrated by the hour
by those who would beguile you
with their lies.

If we warn you of their hidden aims
then rest assured that our claims
are firmly based on fact.
We hold the key to truth.
We live in a democracy,
our press is free
and fed by the greater good,
not power and wealth
or preservation of the status quo.

You are our people,
we are your servants.
It's important that you know this.
The world is yours and we protect it.

Just trust us.

#REFUGEESWELCOME

Blame the wretched and the helpless;
you know they can't fight back.
Blame the traumatised and brutalised
for everything you lack.
Blame the people in most need
for whatever trouble comes.
Don't blame people with the power,
because they can feed you crumbs.

THE REAL MESSAGE OF THE HARRY POTTER STORY

Harry was a good kid.
Most would have flipped
living in his circumstances
but Harry remained grounded,
your normal boy next door
when he wasn't talking to sodding snakes,
flying broomsticks,
doing those things most people can't.
And even if he did inflate his aunt
he remained a force for good,
defeating dark forces like only he could.

Hermione was a know-it-all,
but unlike most know-it-alls
she really knew it all.
Clever, loyal, magical.
But Muggleborn,
a regular target of Malfoy's scorn.

Described as the greatest witch of her time.
She was indeed a witch
but her parents were scarier.
They had no magic tricks
but were dedicated dentists,
the pair of them.

Voldemort was the bad guy,
the Dark Lord,
everyone so overawed
they dared not speak his name.
But he was lame
and Harry was charged with the task
of defeating his evil guile,
a task he gladly grasped
though it was a lot to ask
of a speccy-eyed child.

Of course, Voldemort died.
Harry thrived and married a ginger.
Hermione too wasted no time,
didn't delay, didn't linger
when her own favourite ginger
put a ring on her finger.
The message is clear.
They saved the world,
were bringers of peace.
And like all the best people,
it has to be said…

They couldn't help but love a redhead.

SPOKEN WORD

It sounds absurd, but not long ago
spoken word was something
I had never really heard
and thought of as an art form,
never knew there was a scene
in which I could play a part.

In my isolated heart
there was poetry, yes.
I read it and I wrote it
but never really knew that much about it.
I had my favourites
whose work would strike a chord,
but was easily bored
by the stuff I didn't understand.

No one grasps the highbrow
if they've never learned the basics,
if peak learning years were wasted
in an avalanche of illness and abuse.

Social skills are poetry
and any ploy can be employed
to avoid an effort to fill a void
when the pain of being different
is an overriding shame.

You name it, it came to haunt me.
It's a bit like being unemployed,
that impenetrable barrier
of needing experience to get a job
and a job to get experience.
Life was the job I didn't have.
I didn't have the knowledge
to grab chances that were clouded
in uncertainty and self-doubt.

My mind numbed
by addiction to prescription drugs –
opioids, barbiturates, antidepressants
combined to control the physical pain
but tied creative thought in chains,
imprisoned me in cells of sedation,
clothed me in self-loathing.

It's hard to remember how I escaped this
but I did somehow.
Ideas learned to walk again
and at the rising of the sun
began to run.

I discovered the art that saved me,
the scene that gave me hope,
by accident. A string of coincidence
led me to an open mic –
a quivering wreck who rose from the deck
to put a voice to words I'd never said,

step by step gaining in strength
until I reached a point
where it all made sense,
people understood me
and gradually I learned I could be
something more than I would be
were it not for this discovery.

Now?
There are people who seem to like me,
people I love dearly
who make me happy when they're near me,
filling the spaces once contaminated
with self-hatred,
beaten, bruised and naked –

Those who understand, who care,
have seen their share of troubles

but have talent oozing out of them
with every word they share.

This scene is my new drug.
It drags you in, it hugs you
and will never let you go.
Addiction brings the highs
without the lows
and for the first time in my life
I'm certain that the drugs are working.

LAST REQUEST

When I've had my days,
please, no insincere praise,
false accolades
and recollections of all the ways
I set your heart ablaze.

If you've shown affection
while I could bask in its reflection
then celebrate my life,
remember all the good times,
keep them in your heart.
That way, we will never truly part.

You will always find me in your mind,
doing what I did when still alive,
loving your appreciation,
how you gave me inspiration,
You'll know I reciprocated admiration.

If you tried to bring me down,
plotted against me,
planted seeds of doubt,
displayed any form of jealousy,
then please don't pretend
when my life comes to an end.

The past can never change.
I felt the pain and rage
at your input to those pages
of the story of my journey.

You found me to be unworthy
and that's fine.
You didn't deserve me,
you didn't get me.
So forget me.

If you must discuss me,
spit your venom. Vent it!
I'm certain if you meant it
no one expects you to repent it
because nothing's changed –
don't let history be rearranged.

So often death reveals
hypocrites who steal grief
to shine a light upon themselves.
Don't be that thief.
You'll find enough of your own someday,
and no one will believe you, anyway.

www.ingramcontent.com/pod-product-compliance
Lightning Source LLC
LaVergne TN
LVHW041549070426
835507LV00011B/1002